ALL EXCEPT YOU

Before you start to read this book, take this moment to think about making a donation to punctum books, an independent non-profit press,

@ https://punctumbooks.com/support/

If you're reading the e-book, you can click on the image below to go directly to our donations site. Any amount, no matter the size, is appreciated and will help us to keep our ship of fools afloat. Contributions from dedicated readers will also help us to keep our commons open and to cultivate new work that can't find a welcoming port elsewhere. Our adventure is not possible without your support.

Vive la Open Access.

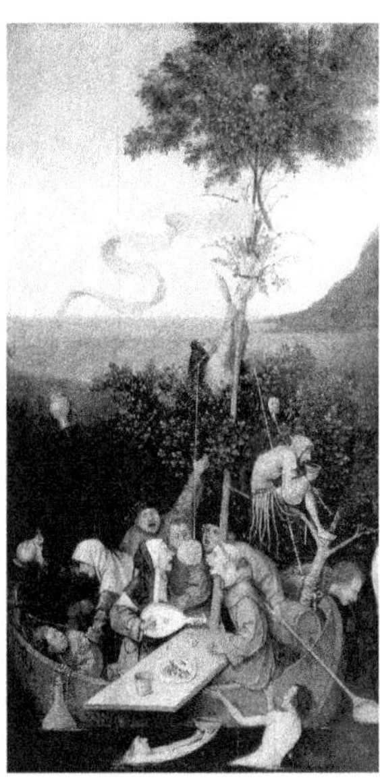

Fig. 1. Detail from Hieronymus Bosch, *Ship of Fools* (1490–1500)

Originally published in French as *all except you* (Paris: Galerie Maeght, 1983), accompanied by drawings of Saul Steinberg.

Translation and commentary published in 2023 by dead letter office, BABEL Working Group, an imprint of punctum books, Earth, Milky Way.
https://punctumbooks.com

The BABEL Working Group is a collective and desiring-assemblage of scholar–gypsies with no leaders or followers, no top and no bottom, and only a middle. BABEL roams and stalks the ruins of the post-historical university as a multiplicity, a pack, looking for other roaming packs with which to cohabit and build temporary shelters for intellectual vagabonds. BABEL is an experiment in ephemerality. Find us if you can.

ISBN-13: 978-1-68571-104-7 (print)
ISBN-13: 978-1-68571-105-4 (ePDF)

DOI: 10.53288/0444.1.00

LCCN: 2023936659
Library of Congress Cataloging Data is available from the Library of Congress

Book design: Hatim Eujayl and Vincent W.J. van Gerven Oei

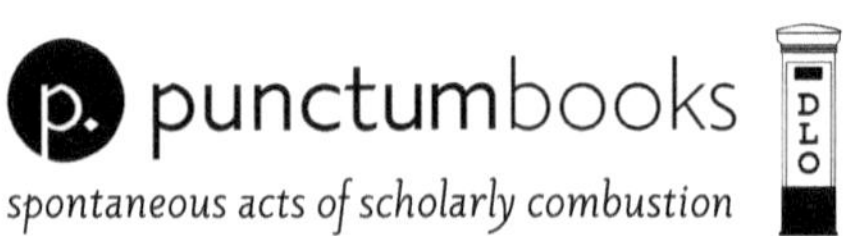

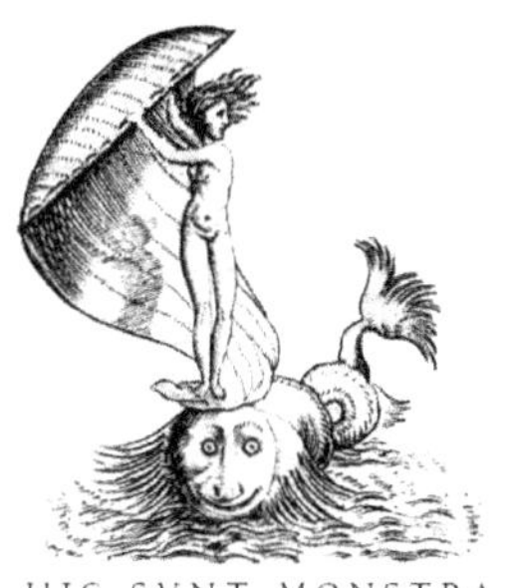
HIC SVNT MONSTRA

Roland Barthes

all* *except* *you

Translated and
with a commentary by
Joe Milutis

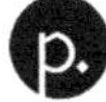

Contents

all

except

you

SIGN

The personages of Steinberg all look like someone I know (I'm sure of it) but I can't recall their name. Who is it? Where have I seen that face, that odd stance? I struggle with my memory, as if in a dream where its precision (and not the blur, contrary to what one believes) makes me the enigma. Steinberg does not reveal a schema; each time it is a figure, subtle and penetrating, who seems to come from my life. In the world of Steinberg, in sum, nothing but likenesses, for which I seek to find the proper names.

"It seems like …" Voilà, the universe of Steinberg. However, because I am never able to go up to that likeness and say what it calls to mind, it seems; it does not grant resemblance, but calls out to me. These figures are at the extreme limit of type, there where the type participates in my life, in my memory. To be recognized, that's the proper role of the sign; but the figure-signs of Steinberg traverse quickly (and surely) the general language of humanity to find my personal language: the idiolect of Steinberg (as the linguists would call it) is also mine. Whence comes, in what is so clearly and overall a *typical* art, the intimacy, the personal complicity. Is he funny? No, because laughter comes at the expense of a type; humor is general, castrating (it reduces); while here, Steinberg and I amuse ourselves with someone whom we have both known.

[*Engage the flow of both Steinberg and Barthes, resisting the violence of pinning down. Words must maintain their multidimensionality, rhetoric must remain a machine, a game. Even the linkage between Steinberg and Barthes is weak, and perhaps that's why this is a failed text (neither Steinberg nor Barthes were happy with the results) but also its power. For that weak connection also gives way to an eroticism. Here the word* type *is used in a way that is particularly French, an untranslatable slippage at the heart of this project. While clearly meant to indicate typography, which Steinberg strains (throughout, Barthes is interested in the space Steinberg inhabits between writing and drawing) it is also a "type":* mec *or "dude." A hookup, anonymous but intimate.* "Non, car l'humour fait sourire aux dépens d'un type"*: Steinberg is not "funny" because humor comes at the expense of someone else (Baudelaire's "Satanic" sense of humor, which delights in someone's sudden abasement). But also, humor creates the "type," it reduces to "type": a generic, knowable character. This is precisely Barthes's "type," what engages his eros. It may be language itself. There's a certain sense here, even from the beginning of a botched connection. Before Barthes can work his magic, he must reduce Steinberg himself to the typical in the same way he quite literally reduces him to type. It seems almost an insult, and may not have translated well. But Barthes quickly displaces this insult onto a shadowy "type" that is not Steinberg, his art, or even Barthes's writing, but rather a shared fascination: a third party who presumably creates the erotic charge that will fuel this experiment. And this mysterious personage is the anti-type, is idiolect itself, somewhere just beyond repetition and resemblance.*]

REPRESENTATION

We can't say that the designs of Steinberg always represent something. But there is always representation in the corner of the paper. Like those optical illusions that change their sense depending on the point of view in which you decide to place yourself to see them, the images of Steinberg lend themselves to a reading in two modes: according to the representation or the abstraction. Sometimes you will think that the representation is in some way chipped by a light delirium of traits, sometimes, *au contraire,* that it is the abstraction of lines that is worn down by the representation.

[*This dance between representation and linear abstraction is of course one of the many charms of Steinberg's work, but here Barthes describes the interplay of representation and abstraction as a kind of damage. Again, a key that that there is some kind of second-level damage that he wants to inflict on Steinberg. Steinberg may be too representational, and the artist that Barthes seems to be describing throughout is not Steinberg, but instead a type of Steinberg-to-come.* "Mais il y a toujours de la représentation dans un coin du papier"*: am I missing something idiomatic in this apparently simple sentence? My instinct towards a looser translation would have it read "But there is always something of representation within the corners of a sheet of paper." But the looser I make it, the more stilted it becomes. The sentence fails to gel because the "paper" is not an innocent entity separate from representation. As in the many Steinberg drawings where the figure opens out, there is an indiscernibility between it and the paper, where the figure is in the act of drawing himself so that paper is not mere representational convenience, but* mise-en-scène *and antagonist at once. What does it mean that "there is always representation in the corner of the paper"? All these figures that draw themselves or their surroundings,* non finiti, *always-to-come, waiting to turn a corner are also of the corner itself. As in the drawings in which Steinberg engages the horror vacui, the corner is a potential space for composition, the far reaches of possibility of the abstract continuation of self—its delirium, extension, and erosion—rather than a framing border. A corner in a neighborhood, perhaps, that can be inhabited aimlessly?*]

THE ALLEGORY OF TIME

Steinberg plays with all the forms of representation; and every form he varies with incessant invention. Here, for example, is his Allegory, antique trope that has survived for centuries; and here the privileged material of *Allegory,* Time that passes. Like all signs (and this one is sumptuous), Allegory permits a signifier and a signified. Steinberg simultaneously switches one for the other: time announces itself (it writes itself) under the successive form of years, seasons, months, hours, or those vague and terrible adverbs that tell the drama of subjective time (*before/after*): and again, the image renews the movement that makes time work, or topples it: river to cross, dotted line that suddenly explodes, unfinished pyramids, column of moments in unstable equilibrium. Yet, across these diverse allegories, a thought obsesses: that of the human subject (the *"moi"*) in relation to which the time passes. The design of Steinberg is at times a *pathétique* (even if, as always, humorous): here, one needs to remember the analysis of certain linguists, such as Jakobson: words like *yesterday, now, tomorrow* are "shifters," straddling the code (we find them in the dictionary) and the message (they do not have sense until I pronounce them): they very vaguely tell the time from a lexical point of view, but very forcefully from the point of view of the subject who regulates the enunciation. Even when Steinberg employs general forms to relate the units of time ("years," "months"), the subject irresistibly returns to the image, in the form of a little person who contemplates, feels, experiences, sees himself a plaything, drawn together by the will of this inflexible procession: it's this small person who always, one way or another, *pronounces* the era, the connection (the kind we make ordinarily across the *shifters* of language) to that ball of illusions and fatalities that compose our "me." The Allegories of Steinberg aren't grand rhetorical machines: these are facetious images of cruel destiny because the prisoner is the small good fellow that I am.

[Not another lecture on signifier and signified! And yet, these are the impoverished tools from which Barthes draws magical effects. Barthes comes from a generation obsessed with "flat" writing. Strangely, he brings it to bear here on one of Steinberg's more "sumptuous" offerings: even the word "sumptuous" I feel must be somehow corseted (and Barthes does so, in parentheses).

Barthes also comes from a generation that was still in thrall of their elders' poetic achievements. Again, Barthes seems to be talking about Steinberg, while thinking of a third party, Apollinaire:

"One day I waited for myself
I said to myself Guillaume it's time you came home
And with one lyric step from out of the void
All I loved appeared
But as for me I was not to be seen [...]
The procession ended my body nowhere in it
Surveying everyone not a sign of myself
One by one they passed bits of myself
And built me little by little as one raises a tower
The people crowded together and there I was
Formed of all bodies and all human things"]

IMITATION

Steinberg represents a postcard. However, the card is itself a representation. The drawing of Steinberg is then *the representative of a representative* (illustrious formula of psychoanalytic doctrine).

This enchaining (generator of images in the second degree) is not reduced to copying postcards. In the universe of Steinberg, all objects represented are themselves representations. That which is copied, in sum, is that which copies. A long chain conducts the stereotypes of social life from replica to replica. To this chain, Steinberg gives a final loop: the chain is stopped, or is returned — not without vertigo — to an infinite perspective of likenesses. Because at bottom, in the final account, nothing: the entire world, from part to part, is nothing but a parade of copies. This philosophy is the same one that Flaubert puts into play in *Bouvard and Pécuchet.*

[*Representation, for Freud, is not representation of some thing, rather a trace of a "deeper" set of representations, which in the end translate the drive. Pure drive, the all or nothing of it, is perhaps what Barthes sets out to understand. Style is, in essence, a clear expression of drive — a personal signature of the artist, irreducible to description, unending ribbon like Steinberg's infinitely looping signatures. This section is titled* "simili" *— deceptively simple word, but rare in French, with a weird boost of usage during the era of French rococo. It would return to popularity in the 20th century with the advent of half-tone images* (similigravure), *in which an image is composed of roughly similar-seeming black dots. Both endless ornate elaboration (the visual hallmark of absolutism) and mechanical reproduction (the hallmark of democratic transmission), attempt a species of flattening and proliferation of the* moi, *which when halted and scrutinized, can easily produce a vertigo, in which everything is composed of nothing but an endlessly plastic same. This authorizes the prescient conceptualism of* Bouvard and Péchuchet: *the mania for direct copying becomes a creative exit from reality, rather than translation of the real.*

Barthes could have talked about Simon Hantaï, Cy Twombly, Jean-Michel Basquiat, Willem de Kooning — all who, to a certain degree, drew a line between writing and image that was anti-mimetic, expressive of the drive. Here instead, the pleasures and terrors of bottomless and total mimesis. The deception of the typical, the deceptive complacence of the copyist.]

CHAPLIN

An artist, popular and refined (popular by "cartoons," which give access to a large audience, and refined by the subtle stage of an entire culture): that's what's necessary today. Because this difficult balance frees the modern artist equally from two opposing hells: vulgarity and esotericism: to assume without constraint the liberty and the particularity of my original vision, and yet communicate with the whole world; to speak with my original language (the one I made for myself) and at the same time to speak the language of others; to please without complaisance. We could call this artist "democratic," and to make it understood by this currently difficult word how much such a position is threatened: by gregariousness which constrains, encloses and muffles, or by the solitude of great innovations. How many artists, today, escape this double danger? The bygone model of this success was without doubt Charlie Chaplin.

[*Chaplin seems not merely* passé *here but positively out-of-place. Steinberg never, as far as I know, drew a* Charlot, *even though his anonymous men-in-the-street have Chaplinesque grace. But are we avoiding another shadowy third party who could have served just as well? If Steinberg was a prominent cartoonist, he was so on the "subtle stage" of the pages of* The New Yorker: *one could imagine another book of an earlier Barthes that would have discussed the "discursive" address these cartoons make, puncturing the prose of* The New Yorker *with intermittent and paratextual square islands, next to ads for vacation condos and French berets. But to remember their context in* The New Yorker *is also to remember the shared fascination that Barthes and John Updike, at that time one of* The New Yorker's *most prominent writers, had for the cartoon—specifically* The New Yorker *cartoon. In fact, Updike's interest in* The New Yorker *was originally elicited and sustained by a letter he wrote to the magazine in 1945 (he was twelve) to Steinberg himself, asking for one of his drawings. Updike was known to admit that he was a failed cartoonist who accidentally became a popular novelist. He could have easily fit the requirement of Barthes's "democratic" artist, however much this "difficult" word would have been contested in the 1970s (and beyond). In fact, Updike was always a little bit perturbed by whatever limited popularity Barthes was gaining in the* US, *in what seems like a mix of lingering Cold War hostility and homophobia. Updike had already written a very catty review of Barthes for* The New Yorker *in 1976 and would write his obituary a few years later in the same pages with the unkind title "The Last of Barthes." Barthes, conversely, was failing at his attempt to write a novel, and in the last years before his untimely death, as with his paradoxical study of the haiku, we find him looking for inspiration in the in-looping calligraphs of Steinberg … drawings (a displaced writing) in the company of, but not admitted to, the forward march of* The New Yorker *"type." Updike, because he was a certain type, found the secret connection between the two. It is the novel or novelistic that really is in question here. So, why Chaplin?*]

THE CAT

Steinberg recounts that in his house he drew his cat on the wall. Afterwards, the real cat would always stay there, close to its image. Reversal: in the universe of Steinberg, it is the image that tames the thing.

(The images of Steinberg are of pets.)

[*In French, the term for "pets" is* animaux familiers: *less of a reduction (to that which is "petted"), the French term retains the possibility of the uncanny catty. We are familiar with these reversals, to the point of domestication. Deceptive simplicity? But if, parenthetically, Barthes implies that all Steinberg's images are pets … the chairs, the signatures, the factory smokes, the cities …? Cats all the way down?*]

TRANSGRESSION

To transgress is to pass a forbidden limit. The frame of the image is this limit, and Steinberg transgresses it.

The images produced for humanity have not always been enframed; cave paintings of the Paleolithic were traced on the very wall; painted animals extended all along the grotto. The frame (to which we have been habituated so well that it seems *natural* to us) would date from 2000 years before J.C. Yet, some artists, here and there, painted transgressions of the frame (in Asian art, for example). In certain comic books, the frame is there, surrounding the scene, but one transgresses it for narrative reasons: a personage calls out to or slugs a fellow from one frame to another. Steinberg draws from this transgression, in his way, enigmatic effects (at once droll and profound: indescribable): an art amateur makes such a close inspection of a portrait hanging on the wall of an exhibition that his head becomes the abstract painting which is the subject of the portrait: the man runs to the other side of the mirror, and yet doesn't break it: he is flattened, as if *ironed* on the surface. The "regimes" of Nature (the living/the inanimate) are transgressed (it recalls a whole baroque tendency, of the which the exemplary artist would be Archimboldo).

(Interesting: the frame is not destroyed, it is transgressed. The subversion of form is not made by its contrary form, but in a more twisted manner: we pretend to look at the form, but add to it a limitlessness that cancels it. Lesson of a new avant-garde, sort of.)

[*Every time I read this, because Barthes does not spell out Jesus Christ, but instead writes J. C., I misread and imagine some forgotten artist, J. C. Cependant, who is pivotal in the conceptualization of the frame. Prohibition against religious images themselves, against speaking the name of God: despite the aestheticization of transgression, this prohibition is tentatively maintained. Despite Christ ("J.C. And yet," "J.C. However") the frame and its transgression continue, even though He makes a border within time itself, which is annulled by His own limitlessness. Tactless to mention Christ in the study of a* WWII *Jewish émigré? Or in the face of the "sort-of avant-garde" of pagan hylozoism?*]

IDEAS

How is it that an *image* can impart *ideas?* And yet, Steinberg imparts them. Or rather—a more precious thing—he imparts the longing for ideas.

[*Barthes, classically trained, is being deliberately vacuous. Image and idea are inseparable in Greek philosophy. Perhaps the italics should be on the word* donner *rather than* image *and* idée. *For if anything the question is, "how is it that image can impart (give or bestow) ideas," since Barthes's original statement inverts the Platonic model of forms. Better put: the "longing" Barthes finds in Steinberg is precisely the nostalgia for outmoded Platonic theories of matter that the anti-essentialist has long abandoned. Steinberg's line chases after an essence that is never attained. And if Barthes follows Steinberg?*]

THE COLLECTION

Like a branch submerged in the waters of Salzburg covered with a thousand little crystals which harden it and make it glisten, sometimes love "takes"; love "crystallizes." Stendhal coined the word to designate this type of brusque and tenacious investment that attaches the subject to whatever object is chosen by caprice. Sometimes Steinberg, himself, crystallizes; we do not know why, but look how he chooses an object (a drawing constraint, for example) and puts it to endless variations: he does not relinquish it until he has reproduced it a thousand times under a thousand forms, in a thousand situations, with a thousand facets: he intoxicates himself with its repetition.

This compulsion is, in a certain way, that of the collector. The difference is that Steinberg is a collector of the second-degree. He doesn't display objects, but the display itself of objects: that meticulous and (puerilely) symmetrical manner in which an actual collector would place them on a table. Thus, the taste of the "collection" (as a procedure and a passion) is at the same time satisfied and demystified (tender and lucid trick, which Steinberg uses to read the world). These flattened arrangements of objects, these stuffed writing hutches make one think of museum vitrines; on the walls of the gallery works are hung; but often, in the middle of the room, small objects are laid out, under glass; in our museums, the vertical is the noble dimension, the horizontal is the prosaic dimension; it is there that Steinberg installs himself: he copies objects which, in reality, would not be worth the trouble, but all the same he puts them in the vitrine: the vitrine, horizontal, functions like a complicated derision of grandeur.

[Stendhal: "In the salt mines, nearing the end of the winter season, the miners will throw a leafless wintry bough into one of the abandoned workings. Two or three months later, through the effects of the waters saturated with salt which soak the bough and then let it dry as they recede, the miners find it covered with a shining deposit of crystals. The tiniest twigs no bigger than a tom-tit's claw are encrusted with an infinity of little crystals scintillating and dazzling. The original little bough is no longer recognizable; it has become a child's plaything very pretty to see. When the sun is shining and the air is perfectly dry the miners of Hallein seize the opportunity of offering these diamond-studded boughs to travellers preparing to go down to the mine."

This is interesting, given the concern of Barthes here with the horizontal and the vertical. The branch is given to travelers about to descend into the mine, a prosaic and yet profound voyage along the vertical. Conversely, Stendhal also describes this crystallization of love (with a sketch that is reminiscent of Steinberg) as a trip from Bologna to Rome: exalted, yet risible linearity.]

TO READ

At a drawing board of Steinberg: 1st we read; 2nd we guess; 3rd ... what else? One feels that a third operation is required, which overwhelms the two others, but one doesn't know how to name it.

Steinberg is to be read, not only because there is a meaning (it's legible), but also because this meaning is multiple, exceeding the letter: there is a surplus of sense, the image (however graceful) is packed with connotations. Further, Steinberg is to be guessed at, because there is always the air of a rebus and what one can't help saying: there is surely a meaning that I must find. I read because there's a great deal of meaning, but I search because there is one missing (the fullness does not contradict the absence: it is the very one that designates the other.)

And then — once one has read and searched — our look is activated again: it is not able to detach from the drawing; it searches and finds things other than meaning. What — or rather who? Steinberg himself, the handwriting of Steinberg, his "idiolect." For this third operation, we lack a word, because it's neither reading nor puzzling out; no language possesses this word; it would designate that action by which we place *art* (simply) at the tip of our pencil, brush, pen — or look.

[*Barthes writes with a blue pen, in a cursive that is both elegant and prosaic. Much of the above seems like textbook Barthes, but it might be better to say that it is part of his repertoire, which he varies and extends, what keeps his writing at play. Alluring dualities, seemingly innocuous, with a slippage. A cup and balls trick — in English the "sleight of hand" (a good definition for writing itself, given the power of slight differences), the "French drop," or* tourniquet *(turnstile). Watch the blue pen describe what has disappeared.*

Barthes has not been otherwise hesitant to invent, import or load words in ways that allow him to recall from oblivion something yet-to-be-articulated: lisible/scriptable, studium/punctum, advenience. *Strange irony: the word for which Barthes searches here does exist, but only as another loan word, perhaps only legible in transit from French to English —* écriture. *While meaning merely "writing" in French, through its French theorization and subsequent popularization (through anti-essentialist theory and experimental writing: Cixous, Irigaray, Derrida, etc.), it has come to mean the idea of script that does not readily accede to meaning, script that carries evidence of the existential or stylistic signature of the artist.*

It is the very thing we are reading that appears to us as this missing thing.]

SHADOW

Here, office rulers depicted on a table; this picture is artificial; in that these objects, minutely imitated, in accordance with a sort of verisimilar comedy, are nonetheless drawn *without shadows.* In myth, the absence of a shadow makes one an inhuman entity, outside nature (the Man who has lost his shadow is marked by the Devil, and the Woman without shadow is sterile). These rulers without shadow, despite their banal function, have something that is bleak, dark — unsettling. But here further on, on another panel, another ruler, an ink blotter are shaded, and the composition is called "Shadows." The title suggests that, from one picture to the other, it is the shadow that Steinberg wants to *mark* (like the linguists say when they establish the paradigms of meaning). Thus is established a *paradoxical* dialectic. The current opinion (the habits of pictorial representation) says that all objects are to be shaded. Steinberg circumvents these rules and takes away the shadow; then he comes a second time to give it back; but it's not the same shadow: it has turned into the *paradox of a paradox.*

[There are nine Steinberg images in the original publication, and Barthes's descriptions are only tenuously related to them. The particular image described here is part of Steinberg's Table Series, not included as part of this specific collaboration. The paradox we have here, then, is not the image without a shadow, but image without image, an image which is shaded through its absence and translation into writing. Whatever uncanniness there is can only be read into the original as somewhat of an imposition. There is nothing disquieting about Steinberg's drawings of rulers and protractors, and like the trompe l'œils *of Dutch letter boards or the trapped tables of Daniel Spoerri, the intent seems resolutely quotidian (we are not yet in the throes of a speculative realism, which might assert the withdrawn weirdness of the object itself). The uncanniness, then, comes solely from Barthes's attempt to supplement these images with a commentary in a faithful light. Yet, no matter how hard Barthes may attempt to trace these images simply, and without shadow (to even, in a sense, be inhuman in the evacuation of subjectivity), there is still the shadow of his desire. His style is irreducible to mere replication of Steinberg and his originals — images which are virtually there (as a mental projection) while in actuality absent (an absence which would undoubtedly have been more profound pre-Google): what is the shadow cast by an image that is not there? As in the Jacques Brel song,* "Laisse-moi devenir l'ombre de ton ombre, l'ombre de ta main, l'ombre de ton chien …," *we move further and further away to give the subject its freedom, yet still follow, somewhat pathetically. Barthes goes in the other direction, not content to be in the shadow or of the shadow but* mano-a-mano?

Further twist: I will most likely be faced with this dilemma triply as I doubt any images will appear in my more unauthorized tracing of this somewhat abandoned text, if it appears at all. An artist might struggle with getting the shadow right. For the writer, the problem with images are their rights.]

ILLEGIBLE

Like many other objects, Steinberg submits writing (by hand) to the principle of *likeness:* he produces a *like-writing.* Still, writing is not an object like others: its substance is one, if not transparent, then purely instrumental, or at the very least always meaningful: writing is not able to exist without carrying a sense: either it returns directly to a message, or it returns indirectly to a psychological disposition: it is an object that is imperatively meaningful, even more than speech which sometimes, by cries, rhythms and vocalizations, does not do what it expresses. In scrupulously imitating this object without, however, letting it be remotely useful, Steinberg makes sense into a "vicious" machine (perhaps which, in the end, sense always is): meaning becomes both a mad desire (we want to decipher at any cost) and a tireless deception (there is nothing to decipher: one knows it, but is obstinate): "I know that this does not mean anything, but all the same, what if it meant something?" This is, it would seem, the same formula for perversion: "I know very well, but all the same ..." Freely offered and impregnable, illegible writing engages a reading that is very much akin to tantric sex.

(The torment of illegible writing achieves its climax when Steinberg designs a seemingly very complex scene and pretends to explain it with a caption written in indecipherable characters. We are two times frustrated.)

[*The word* simili *appears again, this time in the coinage* simili-écriture. *This "it-seems-like-writing" is subversive because Barthes attempts to turn this optics back onto all writing. What is the difference, after all, between the like-writing of Steinberg and the like-writing we call analogy, which undergirds the sense-making operations of language?*

Like Kristeva, who asks "is not exactly language our ultimate and inseparable fetish?"[1] *he uses Freud's essay on fetishism to collapse this distinction between sense and nonsense. But if the mode by which we perceive like-writing is "like" Freud's conceptualization of fetishism, there is a further twist, a triple frustration (leading to an even more heightened eroticism) in Barthes's clearer captioning of the doubly indecipherable. If Freud claims that fetishism is a psychic mechanism to ward off homosexuality, we might say Barthes maintains what would be a contradiction (to Freud) of a queer fetishist. But we could also hold true to the Freudian formulation. Barthes is not technically a fetishist because rather than be traumatized by the emptiness of language, he advertises the emptiness. As one says, he performs it and seeks it out. It is pure "camptiness." Given he is still writing, believing (ironically?) the meaning and value of what he writes, inflating and deflating the sense of Steinberg like a cartoon thought balloon, isn't this nevertheless* the same thing *as fetishism? With this difference: the erasure of differences. What upsets the psychic economy of writing is the subversion of total imitation.*

We could also translate simili-écriture *as "homo-writing."*]

MASKS

Some masks: some would say totems. But the god represented here is Stereotype (of Dog, of Spaniard, etc.), as if Stereotype were the Grand Manitou of our society, and Steinberg its absolutely heretical sorcerer.

[The shamanic mask as stereotype. This small bit reminds me of the affinities the Steinbergian drawing has with the philosophical doodles of Gilles Deleuze and Félix Guattari, whose aim is to disrupt faciality itself, its racist function. There are doodles for terrestrial signifying despotic faces, maritime subjective authoritarian faces, Christ-faces, probe-heads. And then there are the lines of flight … a twittering Paul Klee or rhizomatic composition of Sylvano Bussotti. Most likely, Barthes (and perhaps Steinberg) are at heart too classical to take this line to its ultimate conclusion; and unfortunately, there is a "whiteness" to their work that is hard to ignore.]

STUPIDITY

Like supreme beauty, stupidity is *unspeakable* (indescribable). But it can be figurated. Often enough that's what Steinberg is doing. See this man with glasses, with thinning, well-combed hair, straight nose that eats up his forehead; he looks at an abstract painting with superiority but without comprehending anything in it. Does his obtuse profile make him stupid? Yes, without doubt; but the thing most stupid about him (deliciously stupid), is his little jacket and petite hands: lucky find.

[Steinberg's drawings are not ill-disciplined stick figures, but rather the line is elegant and schooled. How would we compare the ultimate stupidity of today's meme drawings? We evince a different sort of stupidity in the face of a work that plays on its own stupidity, or are we caught up in a completely new intelligence? More stupid, perhaps, is the one who draws the cruel line between the stupid and intelligent. ARE YA WINNING SON? *Deliciously stupid: the father's pork pie hat, the slump of his son at the computer.]*

REBUS

De rebus quae geruntur: there are things that happen that you don't know about and I'm going to make you guess: for example, that 5 and 2 make love on a bed, or that the letters of the alphabet walk through a house, entering through one door and leaving another. The rebuses that, in the old days, one found in children's books—composed in a graphic style reminiscent of Steinberg's—are not solely riddles which excite the mind; they are compositions driving the grand marriage of letter and image that has always haunted baroque artists. The letter and the drawing are of the same origin: on cave walls, before there were analogical figurations of animals, there had been simple rhythmic incisions, in which the abstraction then drifted towards image or towards word: a cartoonist can't but be fascinated by the word and a graphic designer is always a cartoonist. Creator of rebuses without solution, Steinberg stands at the intersection of three practices: riddler (the Sphinx), geometrician (creator of lines), and scribe.

[de rebus quae geruntur: *he immediately translates the Latin into* il y a des choses qui se passent. *The Latin name, it turns out, is a genre of puzzle developed by Picardy priests and the origin of the modern rebus in the 1500s. An old etymological study tells us that we use the plural ablative of the Latin* res *(thing) for this genre precisely because of the name given these Picardy drawings (they are de rebus). A more literal translation of* de rebus quae geruntur *(taking into account the medieval Latin use of de) might be "Those (things) translated from things."*

Why did these images haunt baroque artists? Precisely because what they implied not for the artist-who-drew, but for the spectator-who-interpreted. Charles de Bovelles (1475–1566), also a Picardy priest and maker of rebuses, would initiate a line of thinking—leading to the doors of Descartes—that for the first time placed subjective perception in intimate rapport with external reality. Not for nothing are the image-word innovations of early alchemy and emblem books precursors to modern science. It's not their ostensible content (allegorizing of natural processes and chemical transformation) but the activity of interpreting disparate elements that makes them precursors of modern epistemology. A training in puzzles supplants biblical hermeneutics.]

BEFORE/AFTER

Literally, what is a "cartoon"? It is "any design destined to comprise an animated film." Said in another way, the cartoon refers to a gesture taken from a sequence: there is a *before* and an *after*, there is a story which has started and which is going to continue. The drawings of Steinberg always involve, in effect, *a reserve of history:* they make you want to tell the story of something which has come before and something that follows. Each drawing is thick with narrative, but this narrative, by an impertinent loop, stops short. This is not without rapport with the succinct (and supremely elegant) art of haiku.

[*How does Steinberg draw history, its before and after? We already saw an example of this in his* Allegories, *which does not necessarily stop short as Barthes implies. Barthes's flat interpretation of a cartoon as an animation cel implies that the cartoon's before and after is already existent, in the reel of the film, rather than transforming under the pressure of Steinberg's pen or Hegelian* Aufhebung. *My reference to Hegel here is not meant to be exceedingly arch. Because what do Steinberg's frequent Masonic pyramids announce if not this spiritual interpretation of history? Spiritual, but with a Barthesian difference, since, for Hegel the Historical Personage must follow their own subjective desire. It is only by some aleatory conjunction that this desire becomes the instrument of that history. And it is this desire that changes the nature of the before (retroactively), while opening up the future after. In Steinberg's sketchy histories and unfinished figures, subjective desire is transformed even in the act of drawing, so that the drawing, mid-line, becomes something else. This would trace the difference between* souvenir *and* advenir *that Barthes incessantly marks elsewhere. Why not here?*]

QUAESTIO

Question: dreadful word: it is at the same time interrogation and torture. In ancient rhetoric, a third meaning meets the two first: *quaestio* is the point to debate, the "subject" (*topic*) that one needs to "treat" (like a mineral) or "beat" (like a recalcitrant infant). Thus Steinberg submits a certain number of "subjects" to the "question"; he treats them in every way, he renews, varies, and beats them (like a housekeeper beating a carpet to expel the dirt), and he doesn't relinquish them until they have been exhausted. The bars, the cats, the photographs, the signatures, the bathtubs, the parades, the documents, and so many other subjects of our contemporary life are in this way submitted to a veritable *work* of invention (invention is work), if one wants to give this word "work" the very rustic sense it has according to its Latin etymology: "travail" is the *tripalium,* three planks tied together on which a butcher would suspend a carcass for quartering. In his way, Steinberg, in a series of various images or scenes, quarters the humans, the objects, the places, to extract the eatable essence.

[*Another unspoken party: the French Academy, arbiter of correct French and interrogator of new words entering into the language. Perhaps one should judge Barthes's "subversions" within the context of this stricter language culture than the more promiscuous American one. Throughout this translation, I have avoided gaudy synonyms for some of his often-used words, because it was clear that Barthes throughout maintains a cool, somewhat technical vocabulary in the spirit of the French Academy, which has historically expressed disapproval of synonymy itself. Instead, each word should mean only itself. Etymological history is privileged over synchronic variations. This prohibition of synonym is, in essence, a kind of autonymy—to every word its own existential profile. While America is more floridly multicultural and democratic, allowing for easy equivalence within the language (gabagool is ham), French language maintains the existential quiddity of the word within its history (gabagool is not even capicola).*

And yet, recall again Steinberg's relation to The New Yorker, *which has throughout its history acted as a de facto language academy (think of E.B. White's role in the popularization of* The Elements of Style). *This conservative, even provincial context—Steinberg is mostly recognized for his famous map of the world as seen from 9th Avenue—belies the profound inventiveness of American language, a multiplicity in practice, with utopian* simili *creating new relations.*

Barbara Stanwyck in Howard Hawks's Ball of Fire, *gangster moll who becomes an unwitting resource for dotty encyclopedists, is the sun of this "other scene" of language, the Gothic art of slang* (art gothique).]

FINGERPRINTS

All at once, sudden infatuation, craze of repetition: Steinberg only thinks of the fingerprint, he sees it everywhere, that is to say metamorphosed into a thousand forms at once unexpected and plausible: the round striated print on passports and police files becomes easel, face, landscape, cloud, hill, etc. From functional object (issue of the gesture in which I affix my finger on a sheet of paper to mark the original striations of my skin), the print becomes a universal form: the signified passes through a range of signifiers — passage which is the royal road of poetic invention.

[*Ultimate index: the fingerprint as evidence of being, however bureaucratic and rationalized. And, for Barthes, "index" is a key term on which converges many of his concerns: the eroticization of singular being (irreducible to the mechanisms of state identification or academic discipline) by way of an indexical style, which for Barthes concerns the impossible paradox of finding the indexical in the symbolic; his fascination (via Charles Peirce) with deictic indexicality (how language "points"); and the little box of index cards that is the primary repository for his writing. But it is a singularity that is not locatable (indexable), pressed to paper, verifiable. Only at play (masquerading as universal form in the symbolic) is this print legible.*]

METHOD

Every artist has their "process": not some trivial artifice that they use—having developed it—to impose the originality of their art, but a manner of walking, advancing the hand, the line, to transform the material given to them: a gestural method, you could say. The "processes" of Steinberg are at once very rich and very orderly. Their profusion falls under that grand classification of forms of discourse that rhetoric has called "tropes." In the work of Steinberg, we find material tropes (metaphors, metonymies, repetitions, catalogues, antitheses, lists) and immaterial tropes (intentional slips, autonymies, anamorphoses); to which it is necessary to add that which no rhetoric has been able to provide, much less master: the tropes proper to Steinberg himself, his performances, his prowesses: these are tropes of *recognition:* the repeated forms by which we know Steinberg based upon a simple line (a mode of pressing, lifting and guiding the hand); in short, there where Steinberg *insists*.

(To what end these processes, this method? If I knew it, or rather—because in sum I know it—if I would be able to say it, I would not have needed to inch along so patiently—a little Steinbergianly—along these fragments. But, without doubt, the end of this method is ineffable: "there is no difference between the ends and the means," said an author who tried to define the Tao. "Barely has one started on the path, and one has traveled it completely"; barely am I placed in front of a Steinberg drawing, and I get the entirety of his work—even if I don't know how to say what I understand.)

[*While Barthes does not alphabetically order these fragments — as he does in his 1973 critical blockbuster The Pleasure of the Text — there is, at times, a thematic bundling that illuminates by way of proximity.* METHOD–METAPHOR/METONYMY–METAMORPHOSES. *Here he starts us on our path by a simple but subversive introduction of "method" into the category of trope. Method creates a third party, inserted in the metaphor–metonymy coupling, that — in recognizing the desire of the subject within language — opens the science of signs to unexpected becomings, metamorphoses.*]

METAPHOR AND METONYMY

The royal roads of human language (as Jakobson has shown) are: metaphor and metonymy.

Steinberg uses this very support, springboard, and pretext, this very *chance* (because Steinberg's art consists of using everything that falls to him or at hand) to create, according to his whim, from metaphor and metonymy. If it be a sheet of lined music paper: here the staves are treated like the grill of a jalousie behind which a couple bore each other: the meaning comes by substitution, a metaphor; there, the ruled lines of the paper serve as background for a silhouette of some musician character: the meaning comes by contiguity, a metonymy.

Combination of the two tropes: Japan is associated with the rising sun, the dollar with America: metonymies. For an American dollar and a Japanese sun, Steinberg substitutes a round signet, a passport stamp: metaphors.

[There is a temptation to psychoanalyze Barthes by going to the web to find this drawing of a couple behind the grill of a jalousie. The actual picture is not a bored couple. Rather, they seem content in their musical collaboration. Who, then, is the bored couple really? It is metaphor and metonymy. Or all couples, always boring in their implicit binarism? In this sense, Barthes's philosophy is resolutely polyamorous.

There are somethings that writing can't do (polyamorous, yet neutered), especially with only the grid of these two tropes at one's disposal. Yet, Steinberg is the appropriate "object" of Barthes's desire, since Steinberg's work does seem to meet his critique halfway. There is a sense that there is a grammar (of repeated metaphorical displacements?) in a Steinberg drawing, and its contiguity with The New Yorker *makes his work a metonym of a literary sociolect, while still being excessive and subversive of it. A like-writing, irreducible to language.*

Theories of metaphor and metonymy have been imported sometimes confusingly, and here Barthes adds to the confusion by saying that the sun of Japan and American dollar are metonymic. (They aren't; they're symbolic.) A better example might be Steinberg's drawing of a face on his own tentatively raised hand. The hand is a textbook example of metonymy in this case. Why? One raises one's hand and it becomes representative of the person, part for whole. Raising one's hand is an affirmation, tied to the rights of the self. It's not passive like a "head" count (another metonym) but active like a vote. It is not a metaphor, because a hand is not "like" a person. However, Steinberg's subversion is this: he forces us to see the metaphor in the metonym, he literalizes the fact that the hand stands for the man. There is pathos in the fact that the hand is not, however, vigorously raised, and the lips (on both artist and facialized hand) do not smile. This is a drawing in the long shadow of the Holocaust. The inconvenient truth of self is somewhat melancholically asserted over mere tabulation or figuration.]

METAMORPHOSES

The metamorphosis (theme which nourishes all cultures) is a type of metaphor-plus, in which is written the force — always *supernatural* — that drives the substance from an original form to its substitute form. The metamorphosis is a metaphor in which is printed a certain idea of time. The metaphor is calm, pacified like an equation; the metamorphosis is on fire, it willingly engages a dramatic illustration of becoming: there is in it a question posed to matter, to the instability of classifications, to the switching of regimes of Nature.

Very often, Steinberg pushes metaphor into metamorphosis: a woman is *transformed* (as in a fairy tale) into an armchair, her body flattened, as if reduced to upholstery; a human head is transformed into a signature; elsewhere, we see the same individual *mutate* little by little, from silhouette to silhouette, from infancy to old age: these are the ages of life. For time is, *chez* Steinberg, an animated puissance, which proceeds in fits, mechanical and troubling. Steinberg pulls from it the effects of a sort of modern fantasy.

[I think here that Barthes deploys the logic of Jakobson's tropes again a little incorrectly. Is a woman ever like an armchair, a man like a signature? Only metonymically. Even the example of the aging silhouette works here as a kind of double metonym. The silhouette stands for the individual, while the individual itself is a metonym for the temporal smear of being, a temporal smear which is also a good explanation of Barthes's notion of the text.

Is there something gruesome in this reduction of woman to armchair? Hints of Ovidean metamorphosis, where the world of Nature is explained by a history of sexual violence. By perverse etymology, we are told that such and such a tree or such and such a bird is what it is, because it was once a nymph who was seduced or raped by a God masquerading as a turtle, then a snake, for instance. Trauma and primordial chaos are memorialized, poeticized, while also being displaced. This explanatory, mythical model is supposedly foregone by the moderns. And yet, Steinberg left behind him a long-suffering wife, an abstract expressionist whose own artistic accomplishments were shadowed by his, and a younger girlfriend who committed suicide in 1996. The armchair reference is not neutral. Steinberg was a notorious womanizer. This fact is dissolved in Barthes's semiosis, without, however, what he calls the rightist disavowal of these links in pursuit of readerly pleasure. It is still marked *(in Steinberg as well: a confession?). But I can't help reading into Barthes's fascination with Steinberg the gay man's somewhat tragic affection for a charismatic lout.*

Perhaps at this point, after the climb from method to the Parnassian problematic of metamorphosis, Barthes must resort to antithesis.]

ANTITHESES

In a very kitsch atelier, on his easel, an old-fashioned artist paints a tableau of abstract squares, à la Mondrian. Or another: on a metallic bridge with slender pillars, a large baroque building with three complicated domes.

The antithesis makes discourse lively, but it doesn't make you laugh; for that you need contrast, well-known motor of comedy. Steinberg traverses antithesis and contrast often enough, but he goes further: he produces a mix of heterogeneous languages, he produces a delicate heterologie, a slightly acidic smear of very different codes; he takes two objects from their habitual context and actualizes them at the same time, in a scene at once incongruous and plausible.

[*Another Hegelian stowaway—antithesis. While I don't want to engage in German intellectual imperialism (real enough), Hegel is lovable precisely because so disliked. When such authors have lost their aura of authority is precisely when they can be approached as text.*

Because otherwise, in this translation-as-sublation (Aufhebung) *without Hegel the distinction between antithesis and contrast does not quite make sense, is a difference where there is not one. This may be the charm of Barthes's* simili-writing, *here even in his move to the hetero-. Everything reduced to idiolect and suggestion, rather than meaning proper. His code switching between philosophy and comics, then not as profligate as today, comes with a queasy smear! (For me, I can't decide if it makes me think of underwear skid marks or Japanese haute cuisine.)*

In any case, a quick diagram: contrast implies montage (similtaneity of heterogeneity), whereas, with antithesis, it is the very notion of the space-time of the montage that is called into question. (A new antithesis retroactively changes the thesis because something has changed in history itself.) From a montage of objects (the humor of parataxis) we advance to a montage of space-times and assemblages. Antithesis is literally a kind of a cosmic pulling-the-rug-out gag (pace *Barthes, still funny!).*

Contrast: I walk into a duck building that's really a bar, called "1974." Antithesis: I walk into a duck building that's a bar called "1974." A rabbi and imam are there. They ask, "What did you do with the priest?"]

ARMOR

Empty armor on a pedestal: what could be a more banal indicator of boring museums (where one drags children)? Steinberg presents this stereotype in its improbable accident, its *scandal:* obese armor. It is like an alliance of words (as we say in rhetoric): the impossible meeting of a subject always thin (the wearer of armor) and an aberrant predicate (a soldier is never obese).

[*Why not a fat knight? One need only to think of Orson Welles's Falstaff, whose armor is both probable (note the pathos of its mended plackart) and fantastic (he looks like a gundam).*]

ETC.

In Nature, said Valery, there is no *etcetera:* Nature says everything, only humanity is given the impertinent and exorbitant power to favor the consequence of things in this lazy appendix that doesn't wish to say anything other than the excuse to be incomplete (so it thinks); still further, this cynicism is pushed until this summary is reduced to three brusque letters: etc.

The world of Steinberg is not that of Nature (far from it!); it is therefore full of "etc." Witness how, by this graphic process, Steinberg says "etc.": he establishes a repetition in two dimensions: from one side, frontally, he represents an interminable cortege of social types (let's not try to define them one by one: each is at once — and this is the clear genius of Steinberg — perfectly stereotype and absolutely original), parading under the very banner of "etc.," and from the other side, each queue, viewed in perspective, goes off, like a vibration that dissipates, not because it stops, but because I can no longer perceive it. Cortege and queue are infinite, two infinities that cross and reinforce each other: it is as if, at a second remove, "etc." itself was repeated, sounded in two different spaces.

[*In Nature, there is no* etcetera, *in Steinberg there are two* etceteras *(moving to infinity). Isn't this the problem with a truly materialist analysis, caught between the tendency — uniquely human — of lazy or dismissive etceteras, and a more attendant etcetera that can only be the extension of the "and"? "And" as "remainder"* (et *as* cetera): *while an impossible object for psychoanalysis — it touches the Real — it is in new materialist thought traced, listed, and enumerated but never quite enters into analysis, strictly speaking. The Latour litany is this type of double-etcetera: concatenation, belying infinity.*]

UPHOLSTERY

Minute figurative graffiti, repeating itself, forms an abstract surface: in short, stuffed upholstery.

(In Nature, things repeat themselves, but this repetition is not abstract: no "etc." Humanity itself is always caught in the same movement: figuration, repetition, abstraction, gregariousness, distaste, rejection.)

[*A moment to reflect on the fact that* chair *in French (flesh) strangely here meets "chair" in English (seat). It is also worth noting the lines perhaps drawn here between French* farce *(stuffed) and English "farce" (comedy). Steinberg's stuffed and elaborate armchairs as a kind of comedy of the passion, or punning vanitas:* voici le chemin de toute *chair*.]

ECCENTRICITIES

That which Steinberg very often puts in question is human sociability: his men repeat themselves *ad nauseam*. This effect is especially strong since the inexorable repetition staged by Steinberg seizes singularities: the bearded guitarists, lovers under palm trees, a painting on its easel, all the postures which we think, in a first movement, are fiercely individual. By this simple reversal (carefully "mounted"), Steinberg attains the character of our civilization: because, to tell the truth, our civilization is full of eccentrics, marginality flourishes there on all sides. Boredom: these eccentricities are never singular; the margins repeat to infinity. Wherever we turn ourselves, we find nothing but conformity: that of the Law, but also that of anti-conformism, even more tyrannical. In a way, that's what the army of bearded avant-gardists parading under the pencil of Steinberg is saying.

[*But isn't this reminiscent of the fact that the French Revolution inaugurated a machine of* simili-écriture *in which it is precisely the individuality of the citizen that becomes a common birthright? For America, this formula is* E pluribus unum *(again, recall the Masonic pyramids of Steinberg): efficient operating system or Kafkaesque harrow? We know that this individuality was not always extended to all, but as an operating system it seeks or intends extension, repeating to infinity. There are, then, two conformities to anti-conformism, lost in this light syllogism or irony of Barthes. One conformity concerns the right of eccentricity (extended to all), the other consists of anti-conformity to this liberal law (the populist gesture), which, while adhering to a more tyrannical law, exceptionalist or cynical, only allows eccentricity as long as it remains eccentric, hidden, unprotected by the law. There's of course many forms of radical conformism masquerading as anti-conformism today; and in many ways, for Barthes at least, this seems to be a question of taste, but also of location. Where is eccentricity? It is not marginal, but interstitial. For instance, Steinberg, at the heart of New York culture, does not easily fit into either the world of art or of writing, but rather remains profoundly in-between.*

Pointed eccentricity of the non-eccentric: Steinberg's cartoons are rarely if ever captioned amongst those of his colleagues at The New Yorker.]

THE SOPHISTICATE

A party à la Steinberg: assembled in a grand salon, the diverse personages smoke and talk: the talk and the smoke are the same thing: they merge in the same phylactery which emanates from everyone's mouth and finger. And as no guest is without this breathing appendage, it produces an acute effect of repetition; and I understand this ontology of repetition to be sophistication itself.

[*I at first struggle with the bizarre use of* phylactère *here because it has a specific Judaic reference for English readers, the small case Jewish men wear on their heads containing verses from the Torah. Additional difficulty: while I can easily imagine the original image (Barthes's description is Steinbergian enough), no search brings up an image in which talk and smoke merge as one, from fingers and mouths of various socialites. The closest I can find is an image of partygoers whose heads are on springs, emerging from ornate pyxides, plinths, and pedestals. (There are two more modest guests in the background, one whose head springs from an iron pan, the other from a simple box.) But these various containers are not phylacteries.*

However, I later find that the French more commonly use this word as equivalent to our thought balloon. Steinberg often repeats the conceit whereby the convention of the speech or thought balloon is transformed, materialized. Conversation: a man speaks a dense array of straight lines, while his female interlocutor speaks in sinuous loops. Each interlocutor's speech is so stylized that it evokes personality more than it enables talk. While many of these images visualize communicative alienation (a haughty personage's ornate speech arabesque seems to hold a plainer man's head as if by pincers), these speech balloons converted into sculptural edifices could be simply an evocation of timbre, a celebration of the immaterial "personality" of sound. From the horn of a tuba player emerges a voluted baroque frieze topped with a modern atomic explosion.

Later, I go back to Richard Howard's forward to Barthes's The Pleasure of the Text *to find him introducing the reader to the word phylactery as is, lending it a more outré Barthesian sense, an idiosyncratic term for fragment or aphorism. With the Judaic sense retained, the implication is that each fragment is a box that contains the whole. Correspondingly, the sophisticate — so its etymology implies — is crammed with knowledge: maybe not a general knowledge, but a self-awareness of the group, its repeated codes. And here we finally explain the usage of this confusing word. In the world of the sophisticate, a general vocabulary of awareness circulates to the extent that a whole room can become a phylactery of its culture.*]

THE EXCEPTION

What is a collection, a parade? It is something that I look at. And if I look at it, I am excluded from it. The spectacle attracts me and rejects me all at once. On the one hand, I keenly feel a movement of solitude with regard to the parade, and, on the other hand, I perceive, from afar, the great peace of everything that repeats itself in order to reassure me that I am not alone. An incessant voice crosses the work of Steinberg; we hear only it, and it says: *All except you.* And from this exception I draw profit and pain.

["all except you": the title of the book is in English throughout the French text. Is it meant to stand for the profit and pain of translation?]

LOGIC 101

All art founded on intellection supposes, without a doubt, an *operation,* which is like the artist's secret technique of sorts. The old master artisans availed themselves of fabrication secrets like this. The technique of Steinberg has for its end the production of meaning (a *certain* meaning, that does not resemble the meaning one expects). Consequently, the general operation that defines this technique and for which Steinberg holds the secret cannot be a logical operation (which is part of this science called logic). It is necessary, then, not as a means to understand Steinberg, because he is immediately understood, but in order to decipher his secret of fabrication — which, of course, will not exhaust the *charm* of his art — , to risk a little course in logic.

When they reflect on that which is a "word," logicians distinguish carefully (and this treatment defines their science) between the *usage* of this word and its *mention.* Classic example: when I say: "The rat eats the cheese," the only thing I retain from the word "rat" is its referent, the concrete animal to which it returns; it is as if the word were completely transparent and that I see through this invisible glass something that moves in the real: the word is only in this case seen in its *usage* (its situation): I situate the word to combine it with other words, I am using it to say something that is in my head or at the end of my gaze. But when I say: "RAT is a word with one syllable," it's another thing entirely; for, there, the word "rat" returns to nothing other than itself, the meaning with which I charge it returns in a loop to its formal entity: the word designates itself as word, it is an autonym: the *mention* that I make of it exhausts its usage. On this distinction between usage and mention depend two opposing practices of language. One is largely majoritarian: when we speak, in the current sense of the term, we only handle the usage of words. The other is minoritarian, marginal, oddball, aberrant: no sooner do I play with a simple mention of words than I open the ludic field of all language games. But the strangest invention is to combine without warning, in a phrase or image, usage and mention. I could thereby construct a baroque syllogism:

"The rat eats the cheese"; yet "RAT is one syllable"; therefore, "the syllable eats the cheese." What then did I do in this pleasantry? Nothing more than to mash one level of meaning against another, as if nothing separated them. Logic demands that we respect, between these two levels, a rigorous relation of exteriority: never should the usage interfere with the mention of the sign, otherwise all logic crumbles and logicians are of no use. One can guess that Steinberg, for our pleasure — most subtle at that — passes his time fogging up the levels, transgressing the barrier of usage and mention, traveling, like a genius disrespecting the constraints of exteriority, from the thing to the word, and vice versa: because here's the thing about this endless circuit: a hand, for example, designs the sleeve of a hand that designs its own sleeve: where am I? Delight and discomfort of the autonym.

[*Another sleight of hand? How did we get to autonym? Remember the triad* METHOD–METAPHOR/METONYMY–METAMORPHOSES. *The ending of this section contains the important Derridean nuance with which the distinction between mention and usage is collapsed when confronted with the trace (method, style, subjectivity) of the author; the ultimate autonym — the "I" — in the metonymic guise of the hand, is displaced, dislocated but not removed, but rather morphs into pure circular jouissance of writing itself.*]

AUTONYM I

To write, to read the output of the productions of their art, musicians are served by music paper—just as the orator, the writer is served by words: that's the relation of usage. Steinberg's musician traces a note on a music staff, which is at the same time part of the lined background on which Steinberg draws him: in writing, he writes himself: indifferent to all logical reason (in which the function is to separate, to distinguish, to oppose), he makes of the staff a usage and a mention.

[*About to enter into another trio: autonym, autonym, autonym. In offering up this trope, Barthes is working against what was at the time a fashionable imposition of metonymic consciousness onto all language practices. In the same way Kristeva totalizes language as fetish all-the-way-down, experimental writers, theorists, and filmmakers insisted on the primacy of metonymic (or syntagmatic) partiality rather than the authoritarian holism of metaphoric (or paradigmatic) unity. In light of Irigaray's "irrational contiguity" of language, everything would be partial or nothing at all. Part, part, part. While not explicitly a return to modernist artistic heroism, the autonym intervenes to counter the possible aphasic nihilism of metonymy everywhere. This is perhaps why for Barthes the images of Steinberg are important. They are not completely avant-garde, they engage the imagistic, they dare the metaphoric: we recognize them, and we recognize him in them. But as a kind of writing, these drawings always return to the material gesture of the line constantly on the verge of liberation from its image. The autonymic line is reflexive, but non-reflective. (Whatever it reflects is not the author but his happenstance.)*]

AUTONYM II

In the practice of bureaucracy, some statements of usage are so frequent — "FRAGILE," "APPROVED," "DUPLICATE," etc. — that we make stamps of them so that you merely need to press them onto paperwork. Steinberg is seized by these statements, insipid and only worthwhile in context, and he makes them into furniture a personage transports on his shoulders: the word loses its usage, it becomes an object that one can touch or handle. Context is the immaterial component of meaning. To touch a context is therefore a magic operation: a miracle, in a way … its solemnity rendered laughable by the imbecility of the transported object (vaudevillian) and the punctilious servility of the little person who precedes to "relocate" it with dignity (ridicule — always discreet and as simply amused — is even more penetrating when our personage transports on top of his head, like enormous and delicate wedding cakes, complicated signatures, letters, fingerprints, all the emblems of identity).

[Sometimes it is hard to resist removing the traces of snobbery in Barthes's text, although it seems there is always a masochistic touch. We are talking of the autonym, after all. But if we consider the constant displacement of who he's actually writing about, to whom (or what) does the autonym ultimately refer … Steinberg, Barthes himself, a mysterious third party or the very thing of writing?

A translator of note has pointed out that moving vans in Greece are emblazoned with the word ΜΕΤΑΦΟΡΕΣ *(transport). Both the words for "translation" and "metaphor" are based on this relocation of word. Barthes has metamorphosed the metaphor into autonym (and vice-versa), so it's he who is the little man who solemnly makes this weird haul, transferring the meaning of Steinberg's drawings from one place to another. But it may also be the reader,* mon semblable, mon frère!, *who carries too much of this immaterial baggage.]*

AUTONYM III

Steinberg of course is very aware of the autonymic process and he expresses it very well: "Whatever I design, that's the design"; and again: "The drawing comes from the drawing."

[Comment de frère on devient père. *There is a scene in Hugo's* Les miserables *where two hungry street urchins look on as a bourgeois father tells his son to throw his unwanted brioche to the swans. We are in the Luxembourg Gardens, while the June rebellion of 1832 can be heard far off. The irony is that neither the well-kept son nor the swans really want the bread, but of course the urchins do, and their presence is not unnoticed. But as if to reassert the order of things, the father ignores the urchin intruders and tries to get the swans' attention by waving his arms at the water's edge. When the swans start slowly towards the brioche, the father says,* les cygnes comprennent les signes.

I'm wary of the smug tautology here, the complacency of the false image of nature's self-sufficiency. The urchins, of course, make do with nature and its image any-which-way, having been introduced earlier in the novel while hiding out in the belly of a monumental elephant sculpture. Once father and son depart, the brothers fight off the swans to retain the soggy bun. Translation: my brioche?]

IM-PERTINENCE

Some personages in the street are seen (drawn) from on high, absolutely on the vertical. Steinberg portrays (he writes) the excess of deformation produced by this shifted point of view.

In the linguistic sciences, one calls *pertinence* the point of view from which the observer chooses to place themself in order to observe language — because one can observe it from many points of view: phonology, for example, studies sounds under the pertinence of sense, and it falls upon phonology, as opposed to phonetics, to study them under the pertinence of the physiology of the organs of phonation. A human body can be grasped under many pertinences, but that which generally prevails (all figurative painting and documentary photography) is the frontal pertinence: the artist draws bodies such that I, an ordinary human, see them, so to speak standing opposite my own body. Every infraction of this universal pertinence is therefore an *im-pertinence*. And that is very much what the silhouettes of Steinberg are: they are sassy, deformed by the look on high, stretched, excessively crunched, here devoured by their very heads, enormous spheres, monstrous, there, reduced to the line of shoulders, arms, feet. By this simple change of pertinence, the artist creates an improbable humanity, all the more impertinent because these beings seem to look pensively from below at the scatterbrained creator who, from very high up, draws them and watches.

(One knows now, in certain psychoanalytic work, the importance of anamorphosis — well-known process of some painters — in the unconscious economy of the human subject.)

[Steinberg's shadows are exact, uncannily so. Again, I cannot find or imagine what drawing Barthes is describing. The Impertinence of Barthes — another trope? We've seen him add shadow to the shadow before, and here, it is given another name: anamorphosis, which blows up, hyperextends, and deforms the image. Traditionally, point of view assumes a stable subject and object of the gaze. But, according to Lacan, the very notion of conscious perception of an object is marked by "some shadow, or to use another term, some 'resist.'"[2] *Lacan's classic description of anamorphosis materializes the gaze (it is not object, but* objet a*), so that the distinction between object and subject is no longer easily operable. "The picture, certainly, is in my eye. But I am in the picture." Barthes creates anamorphoses where there are none, blurring what are very clear images, precisely to highlight the role of his impertinent desire.]*

CHANGING PROPORTIONS

Anamorphosis consists of changing proportions. Steinberg does it ceaselessly, because he knows well that all the *intelligence* of an image comes from its deformation (that which is *exact* is unintelligible). But sometimes he makes of his modification a kind of exemplary exercise, and here's a demonstration: a photograph shows big tubes coming out of a terrace: drawing at the bottom of these very real tubes (photography is the "proof" of the real) automobiles, roundabouts, lampposts, Steinberg turns terrace into the walk of an esplanade; smokestacks become kiosks, the tubes form a baroque palace. By the same process, a plate of vegetables sculpted out of silver is the sacred central monument of a place: around it, automobiles and passersby, and far off an entire urban landscape; elsewhere, a music cabinet becomes a building, a banking fortress; elsewhere still, a small excavation made by workers in a gutter, like one draws around a house, a parking lot, becomes an enormous crater in the city. All these changes of sense are only possible because Steinberg *crunches* one against the other, without warning, two languages: the one, as mentioned, of photography, and that of drawing; the drawing appears then like a magic operator who transforms the world with the whim of a demiurge, the artist. This is obviously one of the constant thoughts of Steinberg: to show the power of the artist: the artist is ceaselessly shown about to change the meaning of things that we think natural; and the instrument of this decisive operation is none other than changing proportions (thus they say that all of Nicolas de Stael comes from a few square centimeters of Cézanne, supposing that we enlarge them: sense depends on the *level of perception).*

[*The most famous example of anamorphosis, and the one described by Lacan, is Holbein's* Ambassadors. *An illegible blot in the painting, when seen from another angle, turns out to be a skull. What strikes me in this context are the ambassadors' roles as French diplomats to the Tudor throne of Henry VIII—undoubtedly an encoded reference to the ultimate failure of communication between France and England? The French diplomats hide their impertinence—a side-eyed vanitas. And supposing we enlarge Barthes's lack of diplomacy?*]

INTER-TEXT

Traditional critique habitually formed its inquiries on the basis of a work's "sources," the "influences" received by the artist: this mania is responsible for many pleasant days of university work. The sources were deemed clandestine (whence the necessity of bringing them to light), the influences were presented like a species of suffering. The modern theory of Text has changed this perspective. What is interesting and pertinent today is not what the artist suffers, but what they *take,* either unconsciously or, at the other extreme, parodically. All the languages of different origins that cross a work and in some sense *make* it, constitute what one calls the *inter-text:* the inter-text of an author never stops, and for the most part it is irretrievable, so mobile, subtle (in the fashion of the moiré effect).

Steinberg, reflexive artist, at certain points in his work, undertakes to expose the *thought* of his technique: by a "process" (ordinarily unexpressed), he makes an "exercise": he displays his inter-text. It's not so much that he parodies, but that he *signs* some corner of the image with a light mark borrowed from culture: some rays of rain on a very modern bridge where some silhouettes pass overtly recalls the famous bridge of Hiroshige from Japanese painting; a small black figurine at the foot of a desert pyramid calls to mind some desolate composition of Friedrich. A crowd of styles pass in this way, as citations, in the oeuvre of Steinberg (Léger, comic books, Art Nouveau, etc.) Thus is produced between two languages (that of Steinberg and that of the cultural Other) a light rubbing in which the effect is the smile: a smile freed from culture without destroying it (and anyway, what is able to destroy culture? On the day I write these lines, we just found the heads of the twelve Kings of Judah, sculpted in the Middle Ages; it was believed that they had been decapitated and thrown into the Seine, in the revolutionary epoch, by order of the Convention, which did not want any more heads of kings, even if they were mythic).

[Decapitation, as an aside. Metonym as metaphor if there ever was one, heads standing for much more than they were — in fact, these Israelites were mistaken for French kings — and a kind of clandestine rehabilitation of his claim in the first paragraph about the clandestine itself. Why not treat culture as a thing brought to light, half-work, half-serendipity: an episode in the history of suffering? After 200 years, these heads find themselves reunited in a light-suffused room in Musée de Cluny. But are these bizarre souvenirs the same thing as culture? Perhaps yes, not because they remain, but because we recognize them.

This little bit of actuality gives us a clear date for the moment of writing: it is early 1977, when heads severed from the façade of Notre Dame were found hidden in a mansion during the process of renovating a bank in the 9th arrondissement: before the death of his mother in October, his own death in 1980, and the publication of this book in 1983.]

YOU CAN TAKE THE BOY OUT OF THE COUNTRY ...

The extreme case of inter-text is the brusque marriage in the same statement (the same image) of two texts (two languages, two cultural references), normally separated by an enormous distance. In this way, Steinberg places the two peasants from Millet's *Angelus* in the setting of a highway tunnel; or better, more subtly, he repeats this famous couple before a group of painters about to copy them to their easels. This game of intertextuality serves to produce a very strong critical category: displacement. Steinberg ceaselessly displaces us, relieving cultural signs of their roots, their patrimony: he gives them back to us, at once recognizable and foreign; he does not destroy culture, he subverts it.

[*The peasants of Millet's* Angelus *appear much more prolifically than Barthes lets on, as a kind of stamp transposed to multiple locales. Further, in Steinberg's series "Six Drawing Tables," the one titled "Millet" seems like a locus classicus of postmodern displacements. We see the two peasants standing in front of an "architectural duck," in a postcard, on the drawing table along with the same image on the label of a vinyl record (in the style of Fernand Léger), a snuff tin, copied and recopied from surface to surface so that the line between representation and representation of a representation blurs — a crocodile approaches the peasants, first inside the borders of the drawing, and then as if entering the drawing from the "real" table.*

While Millet's peasants remain remarkably and dutifully themselves from displacement to displacement, like the heads of the Kings of Judah, is their displacement the real subject? Or is it the notion that the land they work has mutated beyond recognition, or has never been accessible to the writer or the artist? Barthes's title for this section is Dépaysement *— shadows of* unheimlich? *— for which I originally kept the simple Freudian cognate "displacement." However, it seems like this title operates by way of a pun, only accessible in French, since "peasant" is a type of metonym of "country"* (paysan–pays*).* Dépaysement, *then, could mean not only a displacement from a* pays *(country or countryside), but also the removal of country itself, and its peasants. Ultimately, then, going against my inclination to translate Barthes flatly and rationally (while maintaining its motion and lightness), I decided to retain this possibly uncanny pun by referring to its more florid American counterpart, "You can take the boy out of the country but you can't take the country out of the boy."*]

A LANGUAGE SYSTEM

Working on this text on Steinberg, I am surprised to find that my notes, my drafts, by turns the arrangement of lines, the handwriting, the erasures, vaguely have the aspect that sometimes a sketch artist gives around the object of their aim: I follow in some way (playing on the word) the *pre-text* of Steinberg. This is nothing astonishing: first because the work of Steinberg has a constant rapport with this bizarre object, half-thought, half-graphism, that one calls a manuscript; and then because the style of Steinberg has an insidious power of impregnation: it is a style that seizes all: the objects and their outlines; nothing escapes him: it comes from one eye and one hand that imperiously substitute ours. Steinberg founds a grand language system in which I am caught and which I inhabit like a space which, for me, very quickly becomes natural. I am bound to be implicitly Steinbergian.

(In the blue lining of an envelope, as luck would have it, after having detached it from its support, standing out against the wall of one of my index card boxes, I see, suddenly, the silhouette of Mount Fuji; I climb it to the crater, then, in jest, from the interior of a little cloud I write — for such is the function of my box: "to classify." Steinberg, thus, gives me license to amuse myself.)

[Je suis happé: I am caught *in language. Translingual homophonic pun?* I am happy *in language?*

But I'm left wondering why he comes down from the cloud "to classify ..."]

TRUTH

The "truth" of a work—maybe the same for an image—is not in what it represents, but in the manner that the representation is driven and affirmed.

It is possible to give a logical armature to this proposition. "Truth," notes Hubert Damisch precisely in reference to Steinberg, "is not of the order of representation, but of the proper name, such as Frege defines it." Reversing the habitual proposition that says that the denotation is the fundamental state shared by signs, while the connotation only alludes to meaning that is added, accessory, we can say that it is the proper name that is denotation; this is what allows Frege to write: "But why, why do we wish that all proper names have a denotation in addition to meaning? Why isn't thought enough for us?" The oeuvre of Steinberg is, if one could say, crammed with thoughts, and, however, this is not enough: there is a supplement, a Proper Name, Steinberg himself—who is the "truth" of what this oeuvre represents, thinks, and says.

[*Confusing passage of a bizarrely twisted binarism, squeezed through non-common-sensical philosophical terminology from German to French to English, but which seems to go back to the basic "truth" elaborated thus far. According to Frege, if we read the sentence "Ulysses was set ashore at Ithaca while sound asleep," the sense of the sentence is distinct from its significance—the latter being that which gives the proper name Ulysses its connotations, its associations. However, these connotations—and even their denotations—do not matter. "Hence it does not matter whether the name 'Ulysses', for example, has a denotation, so long that we receive the poem as a work of art, so it is the search and desire for truth that pushes us to move from meaning to denotation." The push from meaning to denotation would be, a decade after Barthes's "Death of the Author" essay, a return to the author: not as an entity, but rather as suffused throughout the work. And this book poses a Fregean puzzle in which Barthes, Steinberg, and the thing-called-writing are intertwined—in an ornate, non-sensical signature.*]

UNO TENORE

One of the proper names of Steinberg is the very mode of his technique: the way in which he draws the line. What it verily comprises, the spirit of this technique, is to drive the line *uno tenore,* without lifting the point. This obviously implies confidence; the confidence implies mastery; and mastery implies in its turn premeditation. The line is thought out a long time in advance, then liberated in a single moment, quickly (or so it seems). All this process (it is perhaps only imaginary) is well known in the *alla prima* painting of East Asian artists (graphic designers as much as painters, like Steinberg.)

As it often happens—we have already noted—Steinberg is not able to stop himself from ridiculing his own technique: since the continuity of gesture is the principle, suddenly the gesture will be interrupted without resuming elsewhere: the drawing will be unfinished, in a manner all the more strange that the figure itself, at the point where it stops, presents itself as if definitive by its very perfection.

[*Barthes has been taken to task for his exoticism of the "Oriental" (his word, under erasure here in my translation) and is notoriously vague as to the specific tradition he's discussing, although I'm more sympathetic of his cultural cruising than most are and the Suiboku-ga, Sumi-e, and Jofuku traditions are aptly characterized in his book on Japan: "Everything, in the instrumentation, is directed toward the paradox of an irreversible and fragile writing, which is simultaneously, contradictorily, incision and glissade."*[3] *But why localize this tradition to Asia, when in fact the very name he imposes upon it (and the heading for this fragment) is Italian? Alla prima is a fairly common painting technique, and we don't need the more poetic examples of Michelangelo's* non-finiti, *Omar Khayyam's "moving finger," or Allen Ginsberg's (Buddhist-inspired) "first thought, best thought," to give us the sense that many, if not most artists operate by way of the energetic, continuous gesture — which, when halted, becomes the finished thing.*

Steinberg's image en face *shows the word* OHIO *doubled, reflected on the water, along with a factory, moon, and uncanny swan who carries on as if it does not get the joke.* OHIO*: look at it long enough, and it starts to seem like the name for a Japanese city. Subtle self-ridicule?*]

DIDACTIC

Study for a billiard player: without the ordinary shakiness of the sketch, the complex position of fingers is immediately apparent: the right hand, motor (its function is to push) drags back like the expanding feather of a bird about to take flight; the left, guiding, positions the cue, the thumb and the middle finger implanted like two crutches, with the index finger gripping, overlapping, immobilizing the shaft. The truth of movement is not realist, it is *didactic.* Applying this to larger and vaguer examples, this is a *study* which allows us to leave behind the particularities of the hand, to increase by an excess of truth the whole silhouette of the player, arched, leaning, crossed straight along the line by which one sights the ball.

[*Anatomizing a gesture: good enough time to take a didactic tour on the translation of Barthes's characteristic asyndeton—the removal of conjunctions and connecting words where "all the logical small change is in the interstices." Barthes enjoys the fluidity of motion that asyndeton allows. The problem is that English rhetoric is more naturally full of asyndeton than is French. Whereas the removal of a connector, conjunction, or article is flatly incorrect in French, English allows. The English reader will find that Barthes has* too much *logical small change, and when he does leave out an important connector, it just doesn't translate that well. His obsessive punctuation is a clearer indicator of asyndeton at work: a directness, leaving particularity behind.*]

THIN/THICK

The line is ordinarily slender. This tendency, by contrast, gives Steinberg's pen the license of thick *jouissance* in his false signatures: one could almost say that they were written with the thumb, while the ordinarily drawn line seems to come from the index, that *intelligent* finger, which shows, directs, clarifies.

[Steinberg has called himself "a writer who draws." Barthes: "In the end I always return to fine fountain pens. The essential thing is that they can produce that soft, smooth writing I absolutely require."[4] In other words, a writer who draws. Whose signature is whose?]

LOGIC 201

Gregarious societies, fragile individuals: this fragility is combatted with a reinforcement of stamps, photographs, signatures, and initials, charged to authenticate that the individual is quite themself and not another. All this material is abundant in the iconography of Steinberg. All those who have spoken on his oeuvre have noted that Steinberg has placed the problem of identity at the center of his work: others appear to me indistinguishable from each other yet different than I: who am I? Where am I?

Identity (A = A or A = B) is the very question of logic.

[*I'm surprised to be reminded that, as a Romanian Jew, Steinberg grew up under the shadow of the collapsed Austro-Hungarian empire. I remember when—based on my own confusing part-Eastern European background—we were told to say we were Austro-Hungarian: whether through some kind of royalist hold-over, or just for simplicity's sake—although, as Galicians my ancestors' ethnic identity was far from simple (correspondingly, my Italian side never bothered to parse out the various and confusing allegiances that comprised citizenship in what used to be called the Kingdom of Two Sicilies). Looking at hundred-year old naturalization papers, the founding of nations is an essential part of how a person's identity is calculated: the date of independence is crucial—in the US, forms from 1914 were dated as year 138. In Italy, you can only reclaim citizenship if your Italian forebears were born after 1861 … otherwise you will be laying claim to a phantom State that no longer exists (and if your ancestors were women, they would have had no claim to citizenship until as late as 1948). On these naturalization papers, it was also important to note whether you were entering as a "citizen" or a "subject" of another country (or kingdom). Naturalization means a renunciation of these rights and allegiances, which are themselves subject to the historical fluctuations of borders and regimes.*

Fragility: the more personal, non-bureaucratic identity that Barthes ceaselessly attempts to wrest from the State. An example: Montaigne's explanation for his amorous friendship with Étienne de La Boétie, "Parce que c'était lui, parce que c'était moi" *(Because it was him, because it was me).*]

WRITINGS

The graphism of writing (illegible) is heavily charged. This refers to a very precise moment of graphic history—because there is a history of writing, paradoxically well-known for ancient times (paleography) and very little for modern times, since only printed literature has retained the attention of historians. This moment is precisely that of the rise of bureaucracy. To the influence of the bureaucratic State (second half of the 19th century) corresponds the growing importance of its scriveners, and this importance is inscribed in the enormous and sophisticated whorls of the signature: when the scrivener says "I," it is the Law that speaks.

Further, these bygone writings very simply say: the past. By way of handwriting, a comedy is played out where it is the origin that is put on display. For no identity without origin: to be "me," a father is necessary, an order that preexists me and authenticates my arrival.

[Is a father necessary? I'm thinking of Cy Twombly's poignant Achilles Mourning the Death of Patroclus: *two gory scribbles, with a literal blood line between the two. Big-hearted Patroclus, constant companion of swift-footed Achilles, brother, father, and lover at once, self-authorizing each other. While even the name Patroclus is quite literally a patro-nym, he has been un-fathered. Menoetius (meaning "doomed might") gave him up, and he was adopted by the parents of Achilles.]*

STAMPS

In *The General Line*, in order to denounce the ravages of bureaucracy in the new Soviet Union, Eisenstein shows a table covered in paperwork and a hand which signs, initials, stamps tirelessly. The stamp is the absolute symbol of bureaucracy. Steinberg plays abundantly with this round and inscribed form, which functions like a reminder of social vanities: legislation, medals, money, etc.

(Stamp on signature, it's a sort of *clamping* of the self.)

[The General Line (1929): *terrific picture, Eisenstein's best I think, often overlooked for many reasons, primarily because it fell out of state favor mid-production, after which it went by (at least) two names. It's imperfectly "clamped" into Soviet history, cinema history. But let's focus on the name* The General Line, *which of course would have been suggestive to Barthes in writing about Steinberg. When does an image become a line, film become writing? For Deleuze, the leap from the visible to the* lisible *(legible), especially in the case of the Eisensteinian montages of* The General Line, *does not deaden the representation, over-clamping it. Deleuze complicates the Bergsonian fear of the ontologically "still" nature of cinema, just as Steinberg might play with the potentially alien and uncreative properties of the stamp. Deleuze's notion of the diagram versus the representation is crucial here. The former incorporates imperceptible rhythms and allows for new improvisations (with the earth, time, cosmos). Montage, then, becomes a practice of drawing rather than depicting. Montage "through the set or the fragments, gave the director the 'power to speak outside real time and space'. But this outside is also the Earth, or the true interiority of time, that is the whole which changes, and which by changing perspective constantly gives real beings that infinite space which enables them to touch the most distant past and the depths of the future simultaneously, and to participate in the movement of its own 'revolution.'"*[5]]

THEMES?

Things that excite Steinberg and to which he often returns: public places, cats, epochs, pin-ups, beaches, the subway, stationery, bars, birds, crocodiles, airmail, abstract painting, Indians, bad taste, vinyl records, apartments, soirées, painters at their easel, signatures, fingerprints, ID photos, bridges, stamps.

This list—for which it's not necessary to find any order or structure—what does it designate? It designates the "world"—the human world, cosmopolitan, such as it "bombards" me with its images, repetitions, and artifices. Steinberg welcomes this world with an extreme vivacity, he makes himself absolutely contemporary; and the critique that he makes of this world is founded on an incessant alertness, a vigilant complicity. The artist, in whom is always expressed a certain solitude of the individual—its state of *exception*—is also the one for whom the world is always present. Steinberg lists the world—the objects of the world, a little like he could become an Encyclopedist: there is in this light appropriation something *luminous* (since we talk about the age of "Enlightenment"!).

[*Barthes is a discreet man, perhaps excessively so. "Discrete" and "discreet" are the same word in French (they are* indiscrets). *Separate objects of excitement, pin-up and crocodile, fall under the same category of desire. Is this a kind of sterility? We have, one hopes, given a clear sense by now of the* élan, *subtle and interstitial, that animates this net of references. Some writers, thinking they are working in the spirit of Barthes, feel the need to load the text with personal excitements and confessions. But a hypertrophied subjectivity is another way to ignore Barthes's great invention and mode of desiring (which he admits as neuter) through the text: surface on which excitements are lightly transmitted, a fluttering of reference. Excitement as a neural spark. Barthes's text is more personal than the personal ("person" and "no one": words which, in French, are also* indiscrets). *Light is already in the object.*]

LABYRINTH

The list of worldly things extends itself all along his oeuvre; at first sight, it is a *flat* enumeration: varied by slipping from one image to the other (an encyclopedia is not a metaphysical object). However, this enumeration produces, in the world of Steinberg, a second effect: that of a place encumbered by heteroclite objects in the middle of which *we do not find ourselves.* That is the very definition of the Labyrinth. It turns out that's precisely why Steinberg drew the Galleria of Milan like a labyrinth, the crowding and extension of multiple goings-on, a petite autarkic universe. Such is the unrelenting discomfort expressed by Steinberg: the world is sufficient unto itself, *the world has no need of me:* "all except you."

[This labyrinth, although a "classical" image, resembles how Barthes conceptualizes the departure from the universe of classical language into the bewildering forest of modern poetry, which he characterizes as "a poetry of the object": "In it, Nature becomes a fragmented space, made of objects solitary and terrible, because the links between them are only potential. [...] The bursting upon us of the poetic word then institutes an absolute object; Nature becomes a succession of verticalities of objects, suddenly standing erect, and filled with all their possibilities: one of these can be only a landmark in an unfulfilled, and thereby terrible, world."[6] It is a directionless drift, in which "there is no mode of writing left, there are only styles, thanks to which man turns his back on society and confronts the world of objects without going through any of the forms of History or of social life."[7]

Is the labyrinth image, however, a compromise, a refuge in which to experience this bewilderment of style and pure potentiality of connection? And what about this: losing oneself in a labyrinth is quite different from not finding ourselves in one.]

READINGS

I have just finished working on Steinberg, consulting as attentively as possible the detail of his work. I raise my head, I reflect, I let a certain interior look act upon me, which is the look of memory. What do I remember? What is the *general idea* I have about this work? —at first thought it is an idea of the *adjective*: I cover Steinberg with adjectives, which are like vibrations—multiple, rapid—that this lively oeuvre arouses in me. I tell myself: it is intelligent, precise, droll, amusing, varied, insistent, ironic, tender, elegant, critical, beautiful, attentive, open, piercing, inventive, handsome, enchanting, etc. The image quivers, yet insists; it is like a sort of language-tingle that provokes me, and this light drunkenness of pleasure absorbs definitively, without exhausting them, all the adjectives that I discern in Steinberg.

Because precisely: I can't say everything, and consequently I feel like I haven't said anything. There is a *rest* of impression, of which my language cannot make itself master. The general idea that I have of Steinberg is then the following: that it is, to the letter, *inexhaustible.* In vain I made analyses, listed the attributes, in vain ran after the being of this art, I cannot catch up. Steinberg is always in *advance* of me. By much? Not by much, and that's here his charm: his work is very clear, therefore very near, and yet I sense that my reading is never complete, ended. By a last paradox, Steinberg proposes to me a relation both illogical and irrefutable: I approach him ceaselessly (where else but from pleasure) and I never attain him (he is, in the full sense of the term, an artist): I am Achilles, who is never able to reach the tortoise, I am the arrow of Zeno of Elea "that flies and yet does not fly," getting closer to the goal by an irreducible distance, since it is infinitely divisible. A mirage, in sum, toward which, from reading to reading, I advance myself and for which the deception is always admitted too late. Isn't this the very definition of *reading,* as long as the philologists don't get involved? I now know what the oeuvre of Steinberg is for me: a text.

[*Text: Seemingly flat word to culminate this summary, but of course it opens out onto Barthes's entire philosophy of text as erotic body, without subject or object, "no more than the open list of the fires of language."*]

TREE

Suddenly, a very beautiful tree in pencil, fantastic and classic at the same time: the exemplary signature of a *painter*.

[*We shall let Barthes have the last word.*]

NOTES

1 Julia Kristeva, *Powers of Horror: An Essay on Abjection,* trans. Léon S. Roudiez (New York: Columbia University Press, 1982), 37.
2 Jacques Lacan, *The Seminar of Jacques Lacan, Book XI: The Four Fundamental Concepts of Psychoanalysis,* ed. Jacques-Alain Miller, trans. Alan Sheridan (New York: W.W. Norton, 1998), 79.
3 Roland Barthes, *The Empire of Signs,* trans. Richard Howard (New York: Hill & Wang, 1982), 85.
4 Roland Barthes, *The Grain of the Voice: Interviews 1962–1980,* trans. Linda Coverdale (New York: Hill & Wang, 1985), 78.
5 Gilles Deleuze, *Cinema 1: The Movement-Image,* trans. Hugh Tomlinson and Barbara Habberjam (Minneapolis: University of Minnesota Press, 1986), 38–39.
6 Roland Barthes, *Writing Degree Zero,* trans. Annette Lavers and Colin Smith (New York: Hill & Wang, 1968), 50.
7 Ibid., 52.

www.ingramcontent.com/pod-product-compliance
Lightning Source LLC
LaVergne TN
LVHW010626100826
845148LV00014B/3130